CGP puts some spring into Handwriting!

Learning how to write neatly is a really important skill in Year 1, and the only way to tackle it is practice, practice and more practice...

That's where this CGP book comes in. It's packed with bright and colourful handwriting exercises for every day of spring term.

And of course, we've included helpful guidelines and plenty of examples — perfect for sharpening up pupils' handwriting skills, one day at a time!

What CGP is all about

Our sole aim here at CGP is to produce the highest quality books — carefully written, immaculately presented and dangerously close to being funny.

Then we work our socks off to get them out to you — at the cheapest possible prices.

Contents

☑ Use the tick boxes to help keep a record of which pages have been attempted.

Week 9

Week 10

Week 11

Week 12

Published by CGP

ISBN: 978 1 78908 543 3

Editors: Eleanor Crabtree, Mary Falkner, Rob Hayman, Sharon Keeley-Holden, Camilla Sheridan and Hayley Thompson.
Reviewers: Stephanie Lake and Adele Lemin.

With thanks to Gareth Mitchell and Glenn Rogers for the proofreading.
With thanks to Jan Greenway for the copyright research.

Cover image and graphics used throughout the book © www.edu-clips.com.

Printed by Elanders Ltd, Newcastle upon Tyne.
Based on the classic CGP style created by Richard Parsons.

How to Use this Book

- This book contains 60 pages of daily handwriting practice.
- It's split into 12 sections — that's roughly one section for each week of the Year 1 Spring term.
- A week is made up of 5 pages, so there's one for every school day of the term (Monday – Friday).
- Each page should take about 10 minutes to complete.
- The term starts off by recapping the alphabet, capital letters and numbers. The rest of the term involves tracing and copying whole words, including common exception words from the National Curriculum.
- On Day 5 of each week, there is a more varied task. This may involve tracing and copying whole sentences or groups of words with a particular theme.
- A typical page looks like this:

The Week and the Day are shown at the top of the page.

Simple instructions are given in the box at the top of the page. Some pupils may need help with reading these.

Pupils first trace over the light blue letters before forming the words themselves.

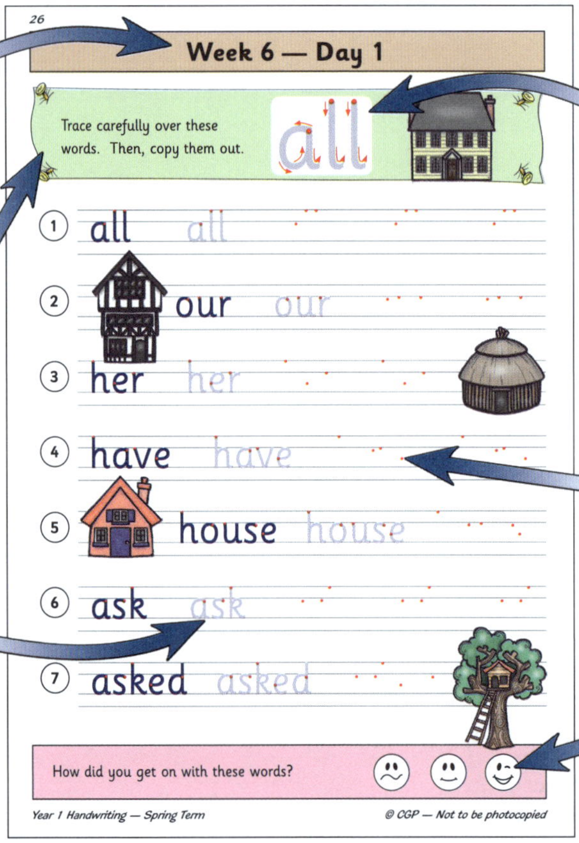

Helpful examples are often included. Arrows give guidance on correct letter formation.

Red dots show where to start each letter.

Pupils can assess how well they've done by colouring in a face.

If you are a parent or guardian using this book at home with your child, you should bear in mind that different schools have different handwriting styles (e.g. 'k' instead of 'k'). You should check with the school to see how each letter is written. In this book, some of the letters have flicks at the bottom in preparation for joined-up writing.

Week 1 — Day 1

Trace each of the letters. Then, copy them out.
Start at the red dot each time.

1.  a a a

2. c c c 

3.  e e e

4. i i i

5. m m m 

6. n n n

7.  o o o

How did you get on today? 

Week 1 — Day 2

First trace the letters, then write them yourself. Start at the red dot each time.

1. r r r

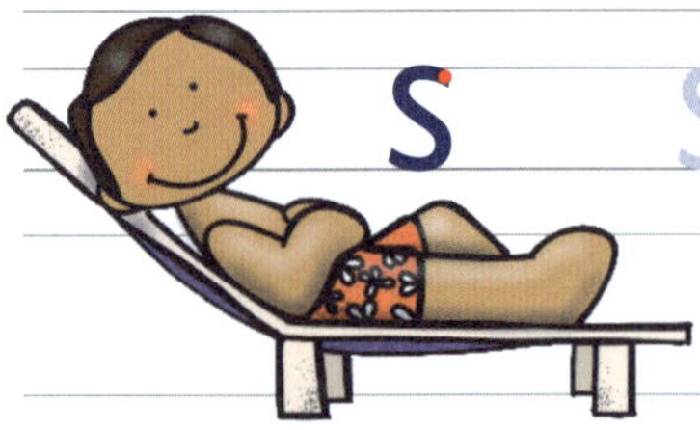

2. s s s

3. u u u

4. v v v

5. w w w

6. x x x

7. z z z

Did you write each letter neatly?

Week 1 — Day 3

All the letters on this page are tall letters.
Trace each tall letter and then copy it out.

1  b b b

2 d d d

3 h h h

4 k k k

5 l l l

6  t t t

7 f f f

Could you write these letters by yourself now? 

Week 1 — Day 4

Try tracing and copying each of the letters and words on this page.

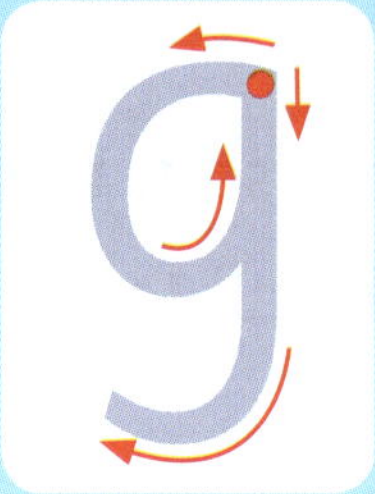

1 g g g

2 j j j

3 p p p

4 q q q

5 y y y

6 go go go

7 joy joy joy

Are all of your letters the right size and shape?

Week 1 — Day 5

Here are all of the things that you need to build a snowman. Trace each word, and then copy it out underneath.

carrot

hat

scarf

sticks

coal

snow

Brrrrrr... how did you get on with these words?

Week 2 — Day 1

Trace each capital letter and then write it yourself. You will need to lift your pencil off the page for most of these letters.

A

1. A A B B
2. C C D D
3.  E E F F
4. G G H H
5. I I 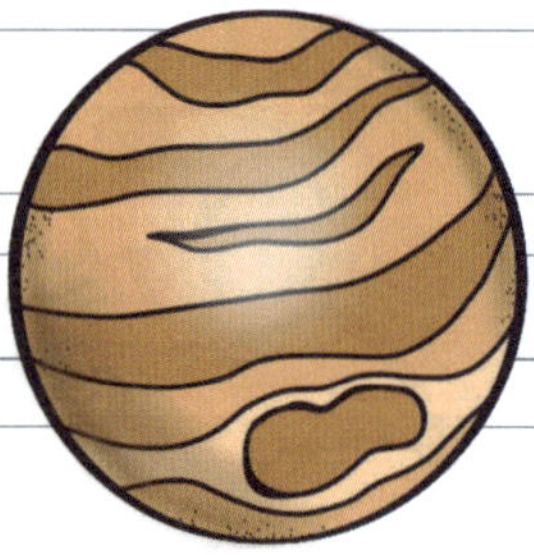 J J
6. K K L L
7. M M 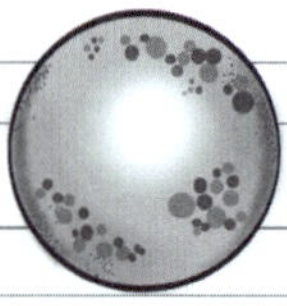 N N

How well did you do with these capital letters?

Week 2 — Day 2

Trace and then copy each of the capital letters. You will need to lift your pencil off the page for some of them.

O

1 O O P P

2 Q Q R R

3 S S T T

4 U U V V

5 W W

6 X X Y Y

7 Z Z

How are your capital letters looking?

Week 2 — Day 3

Trace and then copy each of these numbers. You will need to lift your pencil off the page for '4' and '5'.

1 0 0 0

2 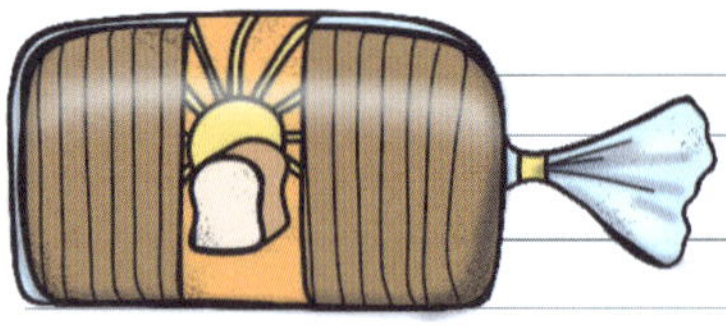 1 1 1

3 2 2 2 

4 3 3 3

5 4 4 4

6 5 5 5 

7  6 6 6

How did you find writing these numbers? 

Week 2 — Day 4

Trace and copy these numbers and calculations. You will need to lift your pencil off the page for the '+' and '=' signs.

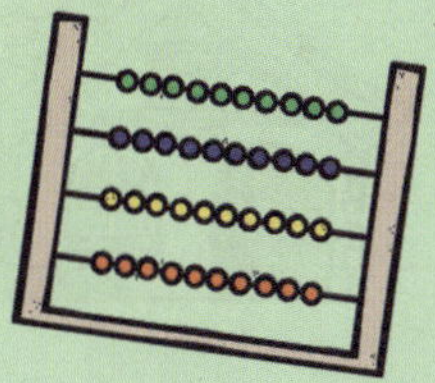

1. 7 7 7

2. 8 8 8

3. 9 9 9

4. 10 10 10

5. 5 – 1 = 4

6. 8 + 2 = 10

7. 9 – 3 = 6

How do you feel about writing numbers?

Week 2 — Day 5

Trace each line of the address on the envelope, then copy it out below.

Grandma Hood

12 Wolf Lane

The Woods

WO34 6ET

How neat is the address on your envelope?

Week 3 — Day 1

Trace over each of the words below.
Then, copy them out.
Start at the red dot each time.

1. here here

2. where where

3. there there

4. come come

5. 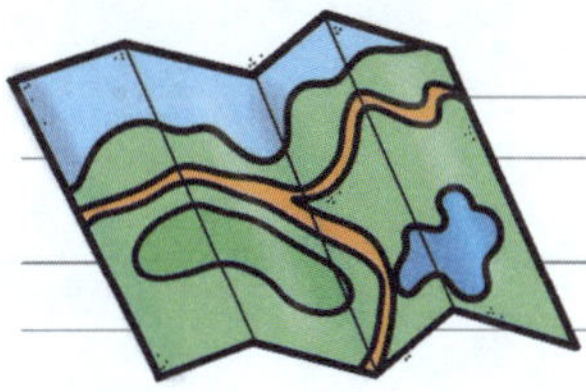 some some

6. once once

7. one one

How did you get on with these words?

Week 3 — Day 2

Trace these 'ch' words.
Then, copy them out.
Remember to start at the red dot.

chat

1. chat chat

2. chips chips

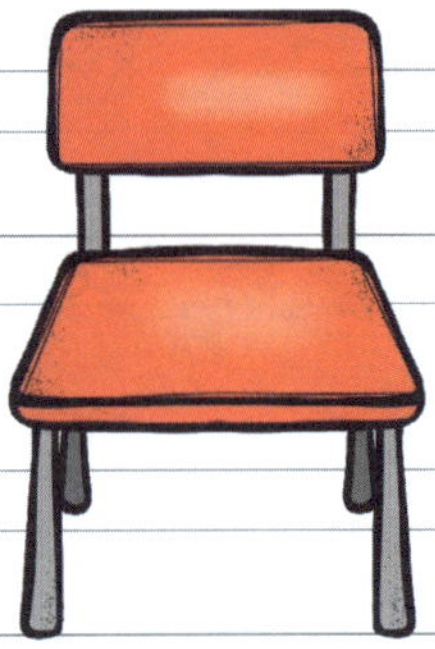

3. chop chop

4. chair chair

5. march march

6. beach beach

7. cherry cherry

How did you do with these words?

Week 3 — Day 3

Trace over each of these 'sh' words. Then, copy them out.

shell

1. shell shell

2. ship ship

3. shape shape

4. sheep sheep

5.  fish fish

6. wash wash

7. shark shark

Did you trace and copy these words neatly? 

Week 3 — Day 4

All of these words have 'th' in them. Trace each word and then copy it.

bath

1. bath bath
2. thin thin

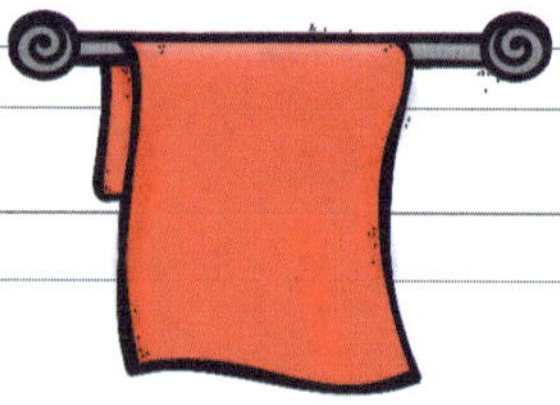

3. thick thick
4. path path

5. think think
6. month month

7. three three

How did you do with the words on this page?

Week 3 — Day 5

Trace over this tongue-twister.
Then, copy it out below.

Six cheeky chimps eat

cheap chips. Six sleepy

sheep share sweets.

Is your tongue-twister tidy?

Week 4 — Day 1

Trace the words first.
Then, copy them out.
Start each letter at the red dot.

1. put put
2. pull pull
3. full full
4. today today
5. push push
6. friend friend
7. school school

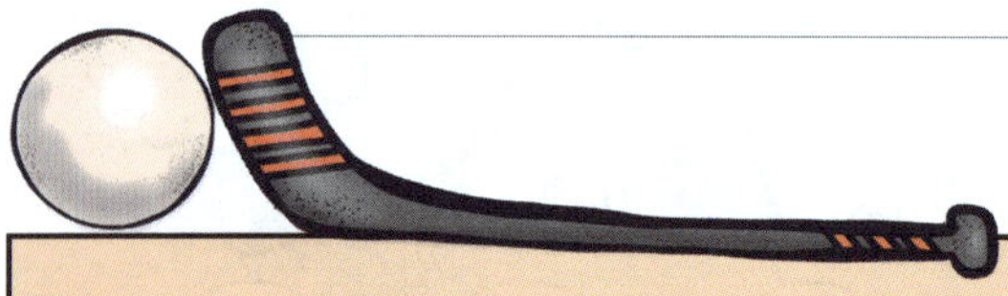

How did you get on with this page?

Week 4 — Day 2

Try tracing and copying these words.
A 'u' always comes after the 'q'.

quiz

1. quiz quiz

2. quiet quiet

3. quick quick

4. quilt quilt

5. quail quail

6. queen queen

7. quickly

How is your page looking?

Week 4 — Day 3

Trace and copy each of these 'ck' words for practice.

kick

1. kick kick
2. luck luck
3. thick thick
4. check check

5. clock clock
6. snack snack

7. pack pack

How did you get on with these words?

Week 4 — Day 4

Trace and copy each 'ng' word as neatly as you can. Start each letter at the red dot.

sing

1. sing sing
2.  hang hang
3. long long
4. sting sting

5. finger finger
6.  anger anger
7. jungle jungle

Did you copy these 'ng' words neatly?

Week 4 — Day 5

Trace over this story. Then, copy it out underneath. Use the lines to make sure each letter is the right height.

Today, the duck quacked.

The chick clucked quickly.

The queen sang along.

The king listened quietly.

How did you find this page?

Week 5 — Day 1

Try tracing the words below.
Then, copy them out.

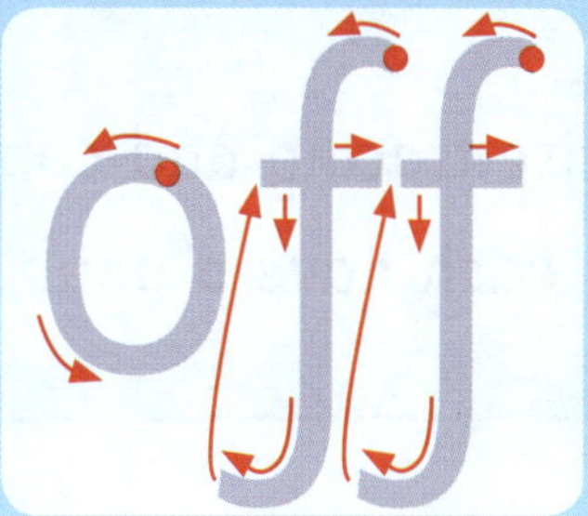

1. off off

2. puff puff

3. toffee toffee

4. staff staff

5. sniff sniff

6. cliff cliff

7. fluffy fluffy

How did you get on with this page?

Week 5 — Day 2

Practise tracing and copying out these words.
They each have a double 'l' in them.

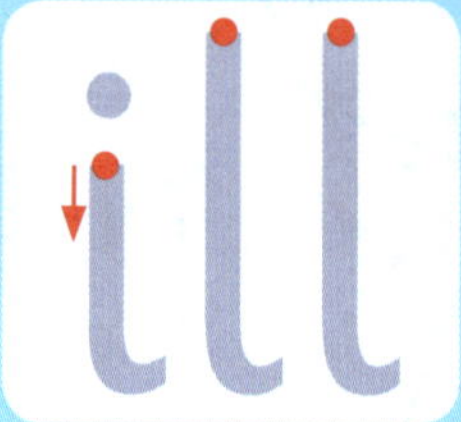

1. ill ill
2.  ball ball
3. wall wall
4. jelly jelly 
5. tall tall
6. full full
7.  shell shell

How did you get on with all of these words?

Week 5 — Day 3

Trace, then copy, each of these 'ss' words.

less

1. less less

2. class class

3. bless bless

4. grass grass

5. dress dress

6. miss miss

7. cross cross

How did you find writing these 'ss' words?

Week 5 — Day 4

Practise tracing and copying each word. Remember to start each letter at the red dot.

fizz

1. fizz fizz
2. jazz jazz
3. buzz buzz

4. pizza pizza
5. dizzy dizzy

6. puzzle puzzle
7. sizzle sizzle

How easy did you find this page?

Week 5 — Day 5

This page is about the three little pigs.
Trace over the words and then
copy them out underneath.

I'll huff and I'll puff and

I'll blow your house in.

silly, cross wolf

small, fuzzy pigs

How did you get on with this page?

Week 6 — Day 1

Trace carefully over these words. Then, copy them out.

all

1 all all

2 our our

3 her her

4 have have

5 house house

6 ask ask

7 asked asked

How did you get on with these words?

Week 6 — Day 2

Trace and copy each word.
Start each letter at the red dot

say

1. say say

2. hay hay

3. day day

4. clay clay

5. tray tray

6. way way

7. play play

How do you think this page went?

Week 6 — Day 3

All these words have 'oy' in them. Have a go at tracing and copying each one.

toy

1. toy toy

2. joy joy

3. boy boy

4. soy soy

5. royal royal

6. loyal loyal

7. annoy annoy

How easy did you find these words?

Week 6 — Day 4

Practise tracing and copying these 'ai' words.

rain

1. rain rain
2. sail sail

3. aim aim

4. main main
5. wait wait
6. hail hail
7. again again

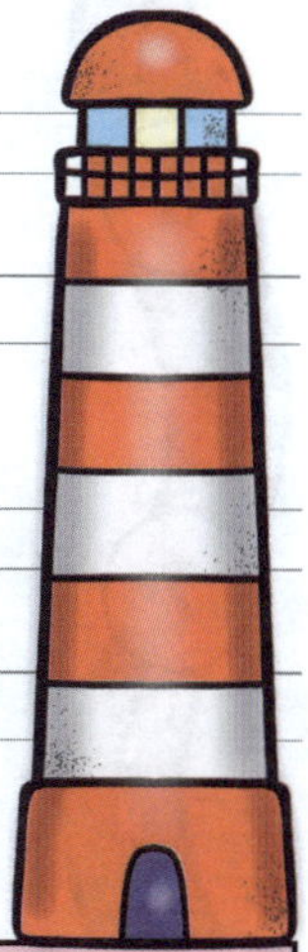

How did this page go?

Week 6 — Day 5

Trace, and then copy, the days of the week.
Each one starts with a capital letter.
Use the red dots to help you begin each letter.

1 Monday

2 Tuesday

3 Wednesday

4 Thursday

5 Friday

6 Saturday

7 Sunday

How did you get on with the days of the week?

Week 7 — Day 1

Trace and copy each of the words below.
Start each letter at the red dot.

1. like like
2. little little

3. what what
4. when when

5. out out

6. Mr Mr
7. Mrs Mrs

How did you get on with today's words?

Week 7 — Day 2

Trace each word once, then copy it out. The red dots show you where to start each letter.

pie

1. pie pie

2. cries cries

3. tried tried

4. fried fried

5. skies skies

6. tie tie

7. flies flies

How do you think you did today?

Week 7 — Day 3

Trace and copy all of these words ending in '-ew'.

new

1. new new
2. stew stew

3. few few
4. drew drew
5. grew grew
6. chew chew
7. view view

Did you neatly trace and copy all of these?

Week 7 — Day 4

All of today's words contain 'ar'.
Trace each one out and then copy it.

car

1. car car

2. bark bark

3. start start

4. jar jar

5. farm farm

6. park park

7. spark spark

How did you find copying these 'ar' words?

Week 7 — Day 5

Practise writing out these numbers.
Trace them once, and then copy them.

1. 1, one

2. 2, two

3. 3, three

4. 4, four
5. 5, five
6. 6, six

7. 7, seven

Pick a face to match how you got on today.

Week 8 — Day 1

Try tracing and copying each word.
Start each letter at the red dot.

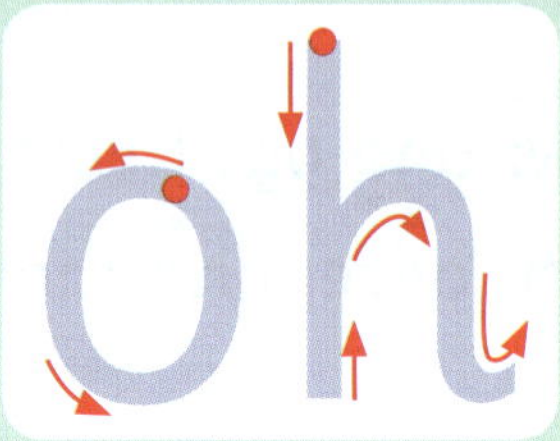

1. oh oh
2. their their
3. look look
4. looked looked

5. called called
6. could could
7. people people

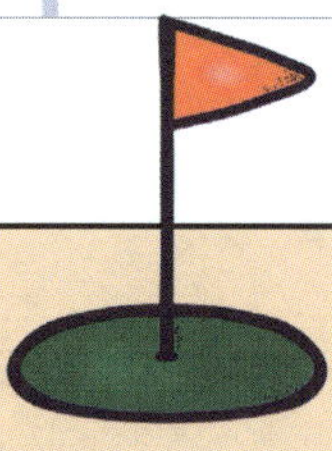

How did you get on with these words?

Week 8 — Day 2

First trace over the words.
Then, copy them out.

stir

1. stir stir

2. dirt dirt
3. first first
4. circle circle

5. birth birth

6. bird bird
7. firm firm

How did this page go?

Week 8 — Day 3

Practise writing these words by tracing and copying them.

claw

1  claw claw

2 law law

3 saw saw

4 raw raw

5 jaw jaw

6 prawn prawn

7  crawl crawl

How do you think this page went?

Week 8 — Day 4

Trace and copy the words on the lines below.

blue

1 blue blue

2 true true

3 glue glue

4 clue clue

5 argue argue

6 rescue rescue

7 fuel fuel

How did you find this page?

Week 8 — Day 5

Trace over each colour of the rainbow, and then copy it out. Start each letter at the red dot.

red

1 red red

2 orange orange

3 yellow yellow

4 green green

5 blue blue

6 indigo indigo

7 violet violet

How did you find writing these words?

Week 9 — Day 1

Trace and copy these seven words.
Remember to start at the red dot for each letter.

1. mum mum

2. this this

3. then then

4. went went

5. them them

6. for for

7. dad dad

Could you neatly trace and copy today's words?

Week 9 — Day 2

Today's words all contain 'oe'.
Trace and copy each one.

toe

1. toe toe
2. oboe oboe
3. heroes heroes

4. goes goes
5. doe doe
6. potatoes
7. volcanoes

How do you think you did today?

Week 9 — Day 3

Trace and copy these seven words.
Make sure the 'e' and 'a' sit
between the two middle lines.

head

1  head head

2 bread bread

3 sweat sweat

4 ready ready 

5 breath breath

6 feather feather

7 breakfast 

How did you find copying out these words?

Week 9 — Day 4

Trace each of today's words once and then copy them.

sea

1 sea sea

2 bead bead

3 beach beach

4 meal meal

5 tea tea

6 seal seal

7 dream dream

How did you get on today?

Week 9 — Day 5

Trace and copy these sentences about teachers and the subjects they teach.

Mrs Sum teaches Maths.

Mr Sing teaches Music.

Mr Air teaches Science.

Mrs Read teaches English.

How is your page looking?

Week 10 — Day 1

Practise tracing and copying these words.
Start each letter at the red dot.

1. will will

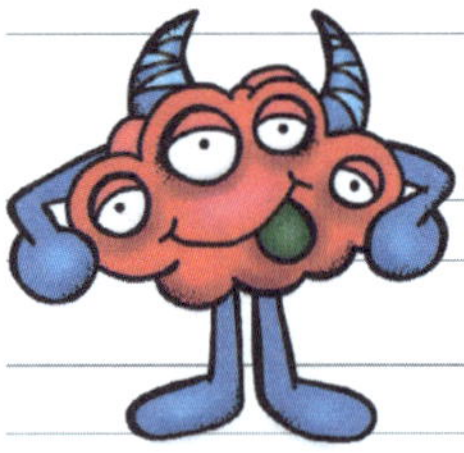

2. see see

3. very very

4. big big

5. down down

6. back back

7. when when

How easy did you find these words?

Week 10 — Day 2

Have a go at tracing and copying each of these words.

rate

1. rate rate

2. tape tape

3. made made

4. pale pale

5. cane cane

6. cape cape

7. tube tube

How did you get on with this page?

Week 10 — Day 3

Trace and copy these words, using the red dots to help you.

ride

1. ride ride

2. fine fine

3. kite kite

4. hide hide

5. pine pine

6. ripe ripe

7. cube cube

Did you copy these words neatly?

Week 10 — Day 4

First trace the words, then copy them out.

note

1. note note

2. hope hope

3. cone cone

4. space space

5. robe robe

6. code code

7. cute cute

How did you find this page?

Week 10 — Day 5

Read this joke. Then trace over it, and copy it out underneath. Start each letter at the red dot.

What do you get if you

cross a kangaroo

and a sheep?

A woolly jumper!

How neatly did you copy the joke?

Week 11 — Day 1

Trace and copy the words on this page.
Start each new letter at a red dot.

now

1. now now

2. just just
3. came came
4. about about

5. old old
6. too too

7. off off

How did tracing and copying today's words go?

Week 11 — Day 2

Trace each of these 'wh' words once, then copy them.

when

1 when

2 wheat

3  why

4 which

5 wheel

6 white

7 whale

Were you able to write all of these words neatly?

Week 11 — Day 3

Trace and copy these words.
They all have a 'ph' in them.

phone

1.  phone phone
2. dolphin dolphin
3. photo photo
4. sphere sphere 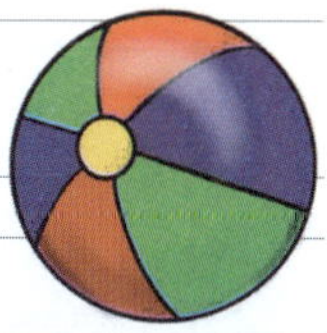
5. nephew nephew
6. alphabet
7. elephant

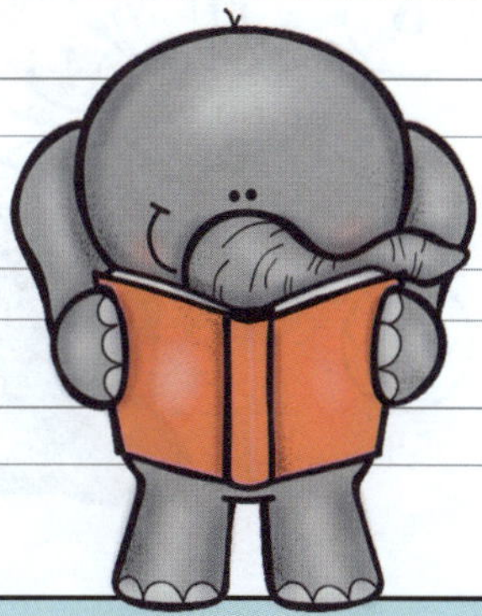

How do you think you did today?

Week 11 — Day 4

Here are some words that end in '-ing'.
Trace and copy them out.

writing

1. writing writing
2.  flying flying
3. sitting sitting
4. running
5. sailing

6.  drawing
7. painting

How did you find copying these words?

Week 11 — Day 5

Here are the names of seven different animals.
Trace them once and then copy them out.

1. zebra zebra

2. lemur lemur

3. gorilla gorilla

4. jaguar jaguar

5. hyena hyena

6. badger

7. tortoise

How did you do with these animal names?

Week 12 — Day 1

Trace and copy the seven words below.
Start each letter at a red dot.

1. saw saw
2. day day
3. made made

4. time time
5. help help

6. make make
7. today today

Did you copy all of these words neatly?

Week 12 — Day 2

All of these words end in '-ow'.
Trace them, then copy them out.

snow

1. snow snow

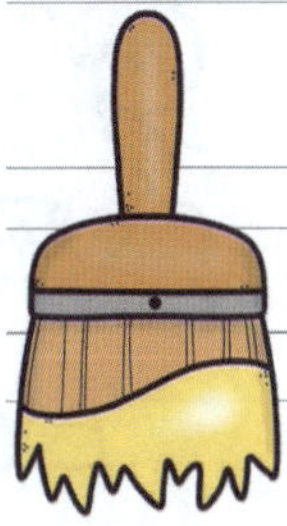

2. yellow yellow

3. grow grow

4. row row

5. blow blow

6. bow bow

7. know know

How did you get on with these words?

Week 12 — Day 3

Trace over each of these 'ee' words, then copy them out.

see

1 see see

2 sheep sheep

3 week week

4 tree tree

5 feel feel

6 green green

7 teeth teeth

How did you find today's words?

Week 12 — Day 4

Trace and copy the words below.
Make sure to start
each letter at a red dot.

coin

1  coin coin

2 join join

3 boil boil

4 point point

5 soil soil

6 noisy noisy

7 toilet toilet

How did copying today's words go?

Week 12 — Day 5

Here are some instructions for planting seeds.
Trace each line, and then copy it out.

1. Fill a pot with soil.

2. Plant seeds in the soil.

3. Water the seeds.

4. Put them in the sun.

Could you neatly trace and copy these words?

E1HWSP11